The Collection

What saves us is rarely what we expect.

Some Sort of Chaos: Poems 2017–2026 lives among the fantastic dreams of desire. These poems explore the moments when darkness collides with doubt, when ambition turns to exile, when recognition feels both necessary and toxic. It speaks to those restless with ordinary life—anyone who's felt big love, failed too often, or burned too brightly to be contained.

This collection is a study in what it means to be alive—
messy, fragile, furious, and free.

Cross the lines of danger
and see how far you can get
before you become nice and boring.

SOME SORT OF CHAOS

POEMS: 2017-2026

JOSEPH ADAM LEE

Red Fox Runs Press
New York, New York

RED FOX RUNS PRESS
909 3RD AVENUE
#127
NEW YORK, NEW YORK 10150

An imprint of The Rebel Within

First edition: 2026

Publisher's Note

This is a work of fiction. Names, characters, places and incidents either are the product of the author's imagination or are used fictitiously. Any resemblance to actual persons, living or dead, business establishments, events, or locales is entirely coincidental.

The publisher does not have any control over and does not assume any responsibility for authorship for author or third-party Web sites or their content.

Acknowledgments
Cover & Layout Design: Eleni Rouketa

Contact Information
Email: joe@therebelwithin.com
Websites: www.josephadamlee.com
Instagram: @joseph.adam.lee

Library Of Congress Cataloging-In-Publication Data
Lee, Joseph Adam. 1986-
Some Sort of Chaos: Poems 2017–2026 / Joseph Adam Lee.

LCCN: 2025922594

ISBN: 978-1-946673-44-2 (Paperback)
ISBN: 978-1-946673-46-6 (Hardcover)
ISBN: 978-1-946673-45-9 (e-book)
ISBN: 978-1-946673-47-3 (Audiobook)

to *Nick Hurwitz*

Table of Contents

Some Sort of Chaos

To reimagine is to admit you weren't first.

The Black Lace Alibi

Women don't give
themselves permission—
unless we give them release.
Their alibi is comfort—
what they seek.
A strong force that
gives them their privilege,
among the halo of privacy.

It's their disguise,
a curtain of black lace,
just enough light
to get in and out.

The nicey-nicey ways,
proper and predictable,
are the killers of women's desire.
They seek not what is expected;
they search for what might
astonish, unravel, or make them whimper.

They work very hard not to disclose this.
It is the secret of their senses.
There's lust in their minds
and logic in their hearts.
They don't care what you think—
just as long as you don't catch them.

Women starve to death
when things become dull,
waiting for the cut—
a sliver of skin waiting to bleed.
They want heat, God damn it,
not some bone-chilling stimuli.
Give them release.
Let them release.
Watch them release.

And don't say a fucking word while they do.

The Candy Man

Hypotheticals expose the idiots,
their inability to read the rules.

Instead, they bend the rules to their favor—
a registration of delusion,
a spark of self-righteous fear,
and even they know
it's all wrong.

They invent authority
to cover the gaps,
ridiculous and particular,
aggressive in refusal,
blind to ideas, people, or quality
unless it mirrors their conditions.

Stupidity makes them small,
and they like it that way.
They live by unreasonable logic—
no legs, no roots, no grasp.
Made up mockery
to pass the time.

And they believe it,
especially when glory is handed out.
They snatch it up
like chocolate at Halloween,
their faces smeared
in the mud of triumph.

Assholes see their indifference
as a brown paper bag,
mangled by loose declarations,
ripping with betrayal,
marking themselves as fools.

They never look at the man
who passes out candy.
Why would they pretend?
He's the one
they most despise.

Dark Roads

The lanes were wide open.
The boathouse was closed.
The pond darker than oil.

Spots of light stared down on me,
hoping I'd say something,
do something.

I ran past them.
Hardly noticed them.

The city was like this in winter:
random climatic shifts,
snow tomorrow,
but tonight warm as spring.

I was alone with the park.
Alone with a lot of things that season.
I never had time to get away,
but I was away.

The road curved with my steps.
The dead ground breathed for light.
I ran on it,
cutting through where the pretzel cart
would stand in April.

It was only February.

The sky's shield didn't matter.
Stars don't shine in New York City.

The walkers.
The bikers.
The ones who lasted
shone on the avenues.

I didn't shine,
but I would soon.
So I kept on the tar
until I was ready
to speak to the lights.

A creative soul costs nothing.
Until it's time to prove it.

The Conservation of Wasted Time

People love the elegance of metrics,
especially when tracking how long something took.

Even when time should be conserved,
we thrift it away.
A plea for meaning—
selling ourselves short.

"It took me three hours to do!"
"It took me ten years to write my book!"
"We dated six months."
"We worked here thirty years."

But when it's over, it's gone.
Time, time, time again—
quicker than it took to get there.

Wasted for what?
We'll never know.

But fuck,
it took a loooonnnng ttiiimmme.

Outrage inspires creation,
but the artist delivers its beauty.

"We're All Set"

People don't keep up.
They give up
sooner than a fish
trying to swim upstream.

Regardless of declarations,
the American is quick to quit—
drowning dignity in the name of duress.

Once, endurance was a sense of pride.
Now, it has become a spectacle,
an audience caustic in bewilderment.

"There must be balance?"
"How dare you make us look bad!"
"You don't include us anyhow!"
"Give us a chance, a turn, a place."

What is unstable makes us strong.
Even muscle must tear before it grows—
and so must we.

We must be torn, beaten, disgraced.
Derision is the invisible feed.
No nourishment other than promise
can sustain one's drive.

Still we eat, in abundance.
We create an image we want to project:
mighty, well-guided.
Proof doesn't matter.

And when it all slips through our fingers—
when the marriage is final,
the kid is born,
the building never built
but the doing continues—
we turn to faith as the next rite of passage,
our proverbial marker of good.

We say God is our moral judgement.
But God is not our family, our vice, or our virtue.
God is the government.
God is the corporation.
God is the slut we fuck.
God is the ledger of our sins
and the redemption we use to forget remorse.

God is the fantasy of salvation.

In this belief,
this celestial makeshift of what we make of it,
to be of the spirit, even in an inquisitive mind,
praising an abstract figure
is as logical as
praising a pencil.

Yet, when asked to write our sin,
we express no story.
How? How can we live without scars?
What beauty comes from the slashes on our skin?

Wasn't it even Jesus who said it so?
Even a myth's intent is lost
in the circulation of followership.

And we see it generation after generation.
The herd bellows on,
a swelling storm of respite,
hiding the moment it's given the chance.

How saintly to live in fear of life itself—
the opportunity of a lifetime,
all in preparation for the end.

But the end is not here.
The end is not near.
The end is a distant thought—
a tossed-and-turned recreation
of the electric zeal
that lingers in the veins of the living.

Not some Sasquatch-sized conspiracy.

We are more than this priority for safety.
We are dangerous.
We are bold.
We are restless—
not for Heaven but earth,
the ground beneath us,
the courage to get the fuck outside
and feel the sunshine on us
like it's the last rock
in the largest lake you've ever seen.

And we sit as a turtle waiting for that sun
to bake us, burn us,
to make us remember:
life isn't purgatory.

It's meant to rumble, rant, rake us
into dread, hope, elation.

So... we're all set?
I hope not.
Fuck that safe shit.

A false sense of reputation
has become our downfall.

Sunglasses in the Rain

The utility workers sat on the stoop
in front of Jerry's food cart.

Drops of nature's diamonds
crushed into small pools
at their feet.

I walked by wearing sunglasses.
No need to attract eye contact
if you can help it.

One of them—
he must have been six foot six.
By looking at the left side of his shirt,
I came to call him Newport.

It wasn't his name,
but the pocket flap was always open,
and a pack of Newports
pressed the cloth to his chest.

I wonder if he ever thought about my name.
My tag said Joseph Lee.
He probably never looked.
I wonder if he even cared.

Hangover Faith

There's sadness in drinking at bars.
It comes from exhaustion.
It comes from feeling ordinary.
It comes because it's the only thing left to do.

We hate knowing how much we can give,
how much we want to contribute.
But the prospect slips
into some burden's demise.

So the misery stays.
The bottle's top becomes its bottom.
We swallow to forget.
We swallow to remember.

Tomorrow the hangover will distract us—
then only fog.
A clear mind is full of dangerous thoughts—
who wants to mull over disappointment?

Back to the bar—our haven,
a respite from false virtues promised to hard workers.
No American ever knows if they've really made it.
But a small part of us believes we will.

And if I do,
I'll never step foot in this bar again.

Hunting for Heroin

The brain is a synaptic highway,
built to problem-solve,
its circuits blazing faster
than the first hit of heroin.

We register.
We dwell.
We see straight through the solution.
We hesitate.
We recite with inquiry.

"I haven't figured it out."
"I haven't figured it out."
"I haven't figured it out."

Figure out what?
It's been solved already.

There's nothing to figure out,
only what you refuse to face:
your faults,
your tasks,
your ego.

You know it.
You keep the distance
from the central cortex of possibility,
from the being
you really want to be.

Fear isn't in the obstacle.
It lives in the self.
It is the hurdle
you trip over on purpose,
in secrecy,
in bondage to the person
you keep being,
the person you refuse,
and never will—be.

We're always standing
toe to toe with our own insignificance.
Scratching the surface
of some made-up reputation
we claim to have figured out,
even if we hate it.

Still fixated on figuring it out?
You don't need to fucking figure it out.

Just do the work.
Do it with vengeance.
Do it with madness.
Do it because if you don't
you'll be hunting hypocrisy.

BE THE REAL DEAL.
Be it.
Because those are the ones
who stop mulling over
the fabrication of fixated figuring.

The sequence of nothing.
Nothing done.
Nothing progressed.
Nothing but possibility's nothing.

Backpedaling on potential,
staying high,
instead of pulling the needle.

And that becomes the obsession,
the Blue's Clues investigation.
Gnawing on the answer,
staring back at the question.

Like a drug you can't kick,
left alone for a while,
returning when the high wanes,
the syringe of sanity punctured again.

Hell—shoot up.
Figure it out.

There's a fine line between
"too old" and "too young."
Toe the line whenever it works in your favor.

Cocktails of Asphalt

NYC isn't for the stable.
Down and dirty.
Tumultuous, irrational.
Hustlers and traditionalists
swirling together
on the rim of a cocktail glass.

The tide shifts each second.
The highest highs.
The lowest lows.
Intoxicated consciousness
washed down with obsession.

I've been dead.
I've been alive.
I've stood on the top of buildings
only to fall face-first
into gravel.

The streets buzz
while the devil whispers doubt.
Still, there's resilience—
the belief it can,
will,
has to work out.

Forever the city of individuals.
Bright as lanterns,
we beam.

The longer you stay,
the more you burn.

Something Beautiful

I'm not sure if I'll ever do it.
Who knows if anything we create
will catch the eye of an audience.

That's where the thinking,
the doubt,
the withdrawal
come in.

Craving a way to leave a footprint,
overtrying to be significant.
Does it even matter?
Will anyone reflect
on something you created
a hundred years from now?

It seems so many try.
We try so hard to create.
We want to steal someone's breath away.
If only we could make everyone
stop and think for a moment.

Possibly we could influence others
in a way we never thought possible.
Perhaps we contribute something
that changes ourselves.

Remain desirous and agitated,
bemused and surprised.
You may find
your morsel of invincibility.

Catching fire only happens
to those willing to be lit.
And aren't flames beautiful?

They are so, so beautiful—
until they burn away into nothing.
Gray ashes lying in heaps
of past accolades.

Something beautiful waits.
Will you be the one
to create it?

A little smut never hurt anyone.

Pebbles

Your life isn't my life.
And there will be times
when I compare the value of mine
to yours.

You'll do the same
to someone else.

For that, I offer an apology.
Neither you nor I
create hierarchy on purpose,
yet it happens.

Comparing is a habit.
Envy— a fruitless by-product.

What we need
is to find value.

So sorry.

Your life is your life.
And like mine,
it matters.

When you're on a tear,
let it rip your guts out.

Walking Blind

If only her eyes
had seen
how much she meant,
we would have run forever.

The Bullshitters Manifesto

People who are bored
make malicious meaning
out of what could otherwise be
harmless, playful, innocent.

They incite fire,
breathe in ill intent,
loins blackened
by cursory social proclamations.

They dive into
what was never asked,
never required,
never meant.

"I watched."
"I saw."
"I know."
Tired mumblings—
meanderings dressed as contribution.
Proof they understand
what never needed dissection.

All for the handy response
to "what did you do this weekend,"
whispered around
the office water cooler.

Thoughts
need not be customary
to the moment.
They can be sequestered
for your own purposes.

The process is slow,
but the payout is grand.
Be one of the few
to take it slow.

Speed spawns
nonsense in their minds.
Bombshells of wooziness—
a pastime for the
lame,
the lousy,
and the stupid.

Assertions faked.
Declarations fall dead.
Regret gasps through their teeth.

"I'm proud of my stance,"
even though they just
made it up.

An arbitrary rant.
Obedience to existing.

They posture in borrowed quality—
the incestuous, unqualified.
Stroke by stroke,
qualifying each other,
lap after lap.

To one group their voices swoon.
To others, they squeal like swine.
Either side reduced to noise.

Selective outrage.
Selective involvement.
Checkboxed contribution.
Was it actually a contribution?
They love conflict
laced in relevancy,
depth dulled by
swift manufacture.

All this censored performance.
What if they slip?
They might say something actual.
Then they're caught.

"I have no words."
Those are words.
And they are not truth.

Find something,
any fucking thing,
other than circling gossip
like vultures over a
political,
social,
or economic cause.

You are not pushing it forward
unless you're sweating it out
in a courthouse,
at a city council,
or inside a nonprofit office.

A march doesn't count.
A conversation at dinner doesn't count.
Anguish at brunch doesn't count.

Nothing is as academic as they pretend.
Most things are bullshit.
Only art makes us gentle.

Your problem
is you keep thinking,
always churning
those cornrows in your brain.
Ignore the noise.

You must earn it.
Ignore the groveling.
It steals your life,
burns your time.
Gnawing on the incision of insanity.

Most live in a mercy complex.
Surviving at the whim of others.
Trapped in the in-between.

Why worry about those idiots.
They never wanted truth anyway.
Too much pressure
to be anything
but ordinary.

So ignore it.
Your time to create is now,
before bullshit drains your verve,
before banality tortures us all.

What Gentle Streams We Vie For

The partial peace of life
is always searching for a gentle stream,
vying as we might to find something
less cluttered, less caustic, less forced.

But so much of life is forced upon us.
We force what we can as true:
the friend who isn't always a friend,
the Sunday gathering we swear is important,
the lover who's terrible in bed,
but better than being alone.

These are the forces we declare must be.
Otherwise we'd go crazy.
And when betrayal snarls
like the dragon puffing smoke in our chest,
we exhale haze more often than flame.

What holds us back?
What makes us stay safe?
What has killed the liveliness in our soul?

The battered life—
the one we all come to know.
Not planned,
but delivered just right,
a reward for doing
what we thought was proper.

How funny when convention is wrong.
The pencil pushing should never have fooled us.
But it has,
as it always did.

"How the hell were we supposed to know?"

As if it were a trick.
As if we never saw it.
The woes of our life
clear as 20/20 vision.
We obscure the view,

force the luck,
hoping to beat the house.

That house of cards is life.
It only takes one missing card
to tear our innards out—
splat on the table,
blood drying before it pools.

And we stare in confusion,
as if we are the nitwit dummy,
the imbecile we mock with
"should have known better."

But when it's our turn—
we play as sock puppets,
no footing,
only a hand jarring our necks,
snapped like twigs in a cemetery.

And we snap,
without restraint.

I laugh about it now.
I once thought it wouldn't happen to me.
"No way.
I don't make mistakes."

But no matter how much you plan,
the branch shatters,
surrenders beneath bats overhead.
Even the dragon can't survive a swarm.

And that's why,
when a gentle stream comes,
don't chance a swim.

You'll drown,
still vying that you were right
about the undertow.

Cherry Sauce and Gnats

You can forget about love.

Like a gnat burrowed deep,
it navigates your core.
No matter how much you resist,
the gnats don't care.

The heart can't shield itself
from being touched.

Love bleeds—
a bucket of cherry sauce
spilling over the side.
She's a desire
too strong not to taste.

What a beautiful mistake.
Weakness comes out of love.
Tears burn the cheeks.
Faults exposed,
fibers of vulnerability felt.

Trusting that love won't ruin you—
but what's wrong with being ruined?

And then there's fear.
Enduring fear.
The bet worth making.
The greatest gamble.

So place it.
It's unwise to live
in certainty.

A plot built on ploys ends in nothing.
True pursuit doesn't scheme—
it simply moves.

Except for Mick Jagger

Youth attracts relevance.
Fresh minds,
cool factors
propagated into display.

Fear of age isn't about health;
it's more emotional than that.

The escaping grasp of youth
is more than arthritis.
It's knowing
the past cannot be repeated.

And still, you try.
You speak of your old this or that—
how you'll rejuvenate.

But wisdom trumps relevance.
Relevance is fleeting.
We all become stale at some point.

Except Mick Jagger
and a few others.

So don't worry.
Don't dwell.
Don't let irrelevance
pretend relevance.

Nation, Against Itself

A country—
a nation where support, care,
and a sense of togetherness
are put aside.

Trained to capture others' success
to divert attention
from those who stand for something.

It's a sad nation,
crippled by self-doubt,
longing for identity,
bashful of its roots,
disgruntled by dissonance,
envious—always envious.

Grieved by insecurity,
helpless without strength,
and scared of the future.

Our nation,
against itself.

Match in the Dark

The first kiss
is the one that does not linger.
Quick.
Sharp.
Struck—
like a match in the dark.

No time to weigh it down
with memory,
or promises.
Just heat in the now,
burning before the city swallows.

But we dare it—
brave enough to step
into the ashes of now,
where whatever we want consumes us.

9:48 p.m., Wednesday.
We cross the bridge.
Brooklyn glows in the glass.
The rain falls.
Cabs hiss by.
Tender as the night.

Her damp-sprung hair.
Her wet-sprung lips.
Her tear-sprung eyes.

She holds nothing,
offers everything.

There'll be another—
there always is.

Gantry State Sunsets

My mind calms
when the day loses its rush,
when cracks in New York's skyline
beam over the trembling river.
I quiver as the orange reflection
peels across Gantry State Park's boardwalks.

Hands latch onto dog leashes,
others fold into each other.
Solo stars tap at phone screens,
anticipating,
wondering,

Should I call him?

I think of her then.
I don't miss her as much as I used to.
The moments we had in the park are long gone,
but the dock's lamps shadow down
and remind me of an eerie past.

The pier looks out
over what used to be our town.
It strikes me.
It makes me wish for us again.
Not forever—
just enough to remember how great it was.

Yes, to remember.

I hadn't allowed myself to—until now.

To Burst

The heart has slowed.
Citizens walk.
A state where running has stopped.

Boundaries feel insurmountable,
outweighing the fever to beat the odds.
Numbers don't lie.
But do they?
It depends.

Crowds move,
togetherness unbridled
by the insecurities of loneliness.
Journeys don't happen without a backbone,
simply, the need for a friend.

But how can one reach
their truest potential
unless they are alone,
unless they have the chance
to find it,
to make it happen?

There's only one chance.
And as much as anyone—or I—can do it,
the beat is steady.
Life moves forward,
safe as bread
rising from the toaster each morning.

I dare you.
I dare myself.
Forget the toast.
Find it.
Something, anything.
Pursue it.

Not for notoriety.
But because we need it,
to know we've found it.
That's what America used to be.

I see my peers
and don't see myself.
Alone.
Distinguished.
Uneasy with acceptance.

And when I feel my heart,
it beats faster,
it pains my chest,
nearly exploding.
It's unbelievable
how close I feel to the end
when I think of this.

And for all my sentiment,
even in these dire straits,
I remember it's my heart.
And I dare it,
I dare it to burst.

She Preferred the Twists

She was hardheaded and hell-bent.
That's what I loved about her.
She was life.
She made me feel alive.

I haven't seen her in many years.
I wish I met her as I am now.

Life starts as a winding road of uncertainty.
There's a chance,
but it hides behind obstacles and sharp turns
that youth throws in your way.

There's hope for discovery.
Navigation becomes addictive,
a drug.

But too soon,
the road becomes predictable.
Wisdom has a funny way
of making things ordinary.

I thought I wanted comfort after a while.
That's when she and I disagreed.

She preferred the twists.
The strange fear of instability was okay with her.

I remember being horrified
the first summer we met.
Even when she slipped toward routine,
I knew it was temporary.
Summer always pulled us back to the start.

Those four months,
wildly different.

I miss my summers with her.

I'll get over this.
A brisk moment of nostalgia.
My head knows better.

Damn it.
I don't like that I think that way.
My head?
Life's goal shouldn't be practical.

We should run like mad,
shouting from rooftops.
I want to look into someone's face
and devour their inhibitions.

Let our hearts pound so hard
the only mode of survival is to laugh.
And laugh we will,
how else do we relieve the pressure?

She always laughed.

I wonder if she still does.
I hope she hasn't lost it.
I hope I have the courage
to find life again.

You can't fear your own expertise.
Leave that to the competition.

Never Still

There's a fervor tonight.
The wind and I believe in the rush.
I run with the soaring stream
and find myself
woven into its wild force.

Big.
Bold.
Brave.

I dare to escape
as air vanishes—
gone but never still.

The Lights of My City

The streets were glazed
like icing on chocolate sticks.

Glowing dreams in windows,
storefronts,
nail salons,
and bus stops.

Lonely patrons
sit behind fogged glass.
The night steams
without desire.

The city sleeps
a winter's slumber.
Quieter
this time of year.

It was all noise once.
All new.

Now it's routine.
There's my Chinese spot.
I should do laundry.
The lights don't excite me;
they don't guide me.

My city's lights
only remind me there's life—
that I'm part of it.

The months pass faster,
slipping by unnoticed,
streaming through wires—
electrified mundanity.

And I see it now:
little moments
turn into little thoughts,
into little changes.

And little changes
are all we have.

Cancel me.
So I can die in peace.

Packed Like Meat

At least a hundred crammed in.
9:18 a.m.
The subway packed,
air thick with sweat and sleep.

Earbuds dangle.
Dead faces jolt awake
at their stops for work.

A man reads the Bible.
Another paperback.
Nobody smiles.
Morning blues choke the car.

Everyone's thinking,
most likely the same thing:
how fast can we get through the day?

Me?
I'd rather be home.

The quiet is brutal.
Will we arrive?
Where do any of us ever end up?

Today is another small step.
Where we go from here
is too far away.

Solving Solutions

I forget,
or at least I try to.
The mounting reasons.
Flashbacks give me whiplash,
spoiled by sour scenes.

But what's so wrong
with unpredictability?

Practicality
is tennis against a wall.
No one really wants to hit alone,
even if the serve sucks.

How easy it is
to make problems harder.
Infectious,
they suffocate.
They'll kill if you let them.

And I did.

I die when I think
about the times I can't recreate.
They can never happen again—
or can they?
All I have to do is make a call.
I don't—
I don't know if I can.
A solution not in need of solving,
but I think it over anyhow.

She and I were always
more complicated than answers.
Our mystery was more alluring.
Sometimes people are best
described by questions.

A solution
would be too easy to come by.

And I love flaws.
Maybe it was always meant to be that way,
flawed.

Maybe solving solutions
was never as hard
as we made them out to be.

All Sweetness Burns

Most people wish
something startling
would happen to them.

But when it does—
they run.

I've been known
to dive into the flames.
I don't know why.
Maybe some of us
like to be burned.

You feel alive for a moment,
until yesterday's embers
cool into ordinary.

How dull, to live safe—
unblemished, untouched, unlived.
Even the yearning for love
can be a death sentence.
Heartbreak is a gift.
We run
just when
it should shatter us.

The fear of fret
is its own small death—
a meaningless circumstance
we pretend gives meaning.
It's the same aversion
that keeps us from the flame.

Let go.
We're all equal.
Because if you don't,
you'll never know
the sweetness
of life's burn.

Distractions replace creativity.
Distractions kill depth.

Youth is a deadly serum.
Drugs just expose it.
Survival is the only antidote.

The Rubber Band

I think so far ahead,
when I come back
I'm angry.

My mind is a rubber band—
widened by curiosity,
other times by expectation.

A yank after
watching a movie,
meeting a deadline,
taking a trip,
seeing the legs of a woman on the subway—
whatever stretches the fibers further.

Sometimes I wake with headaches,
the band pulled too tight,
taut, near bursting.

But it can always be pulled more,
and that's the crime against myself—
to think it has no limits.

Yet it does.
When it dries,
brittle along the line,
it snaps.

But I've come too far
to waste it on regret.

Besides, rubber bands are a dime a dozen.

Down the Hatch

Art is no longer
about uncovering a feeling—
it's manufactured
to match the metrics.

Made cheap.
Made easy.
Marketing plump.
Down the hatch it goes.

We are conditioned
to call it organic,
to swear it's truth—
an amalgam of trends.

Fads, fashions,
faces on loan—
artists who don't even
create their own art.

Fraud applauds fraud.

Inevitably, everyone spends their future
trying to recreate the past.

Beautiful People on Rainy Days

Raindrops tiptoe beside me.
Small tears slip into gutters,
temporary swimming pools for rats.

Boots—
green,
yellow,
polka-dot.

A hunched back spoons
a polyester shield.
There's Al.
His belly folds over
a sweatpant waistband.
His T-shirt doesn't stand a chance.
He smokes, takes one last drag,
flicks it into my line of sight.

I watch the smolder suffocate.
I put it out of its misery.
Flattened cigarette butts surround me.
Sherry will sweep them up Sunday,
that's trash day.

The chain-link fence
outside Apartment 47
blinks back.
I finger the ridges,
cold, wet.
Oddly comforting.

Until it's over.
I look down 34th Street.
Turtle shells bounce—
black and blue,
orb-like.

The rain isn't even that bad.
Umbrellas are accessories,
like watches, purses, rings.
The streets remind me—
inadequacy is survival.

I think back to Al.
Maybe he's got it figured out.
Let the belly hang.
No coverage needed.
Perfectly fine
passing time,
watching the drops,
watching the smoke,
watching his ordinary life
drift by.

Stature of Statues

All the people you meet,
until you outbeat them
in every way they thought
you'd stay the same.

When friend turns to foe,
when pleasantries hide undercurrents,
when smooth civility
becomes rough-edge cuts.

That's how it always is.

They preach potential,
but proof eludes them.

The creatives,
the doers,
the ones we praise from a distance.
Until we become them.

Then we are outcast—
for being right,
for being bold,
for being beautiful.

While the ugly and ordinary
congregate to pull us down
as we pull up.

Stature alone—
a symbol of resilience.
But even statues are torn down
when enough people claim to see a villain.

That secret we all keep.
But what good is evil
if we all hold it in?

How do we disguise the hero?
Isn't he, too,
living with the devil inside?

We carry fear in our faces,
to do right,
even if obedience kills us.
And it will.
It always has.

But we nod in agreement,
to the last pledge of allegiance,
to the wasteland of our woes.

And then we cry.

Because if only we could be the villain,
at least we might be
one among the statues.

To Be Seen, Not Solved

Women complain
because they want recognition.

Their daily struggle and strife,
a routine born from the morning's conundrum,
an inverted plea for acknowledgment.

Waiting for the call:
"You do sooooo much."
"That poooor woman."

We dumb men
offer a solution.
She says,
"You don't get it."

She doesn't want the solution.
She wants the praise for her struggle—
regardless if she adds to it.
Same tomorrow.
Same the next day.

She just wants the credit,
not the fix.
Because the fix sounds like:
"Well, you should know better, dummy."

Women are fragile.
They want to be liked—
even more so
by their worst enemies.

Deep down she's scared,
a little fraidy-baby
to do anything else.
She resides in the issue of the day,
like a caterpillar in her cocoon.

Hence the search
for daily conundrums
that define her struggle:

"Phew, I have something to deal with—
so no one can say I'm not contributing."

But even she knows
what she's immersed in
amounts to very little.
But it's hers,
she defends it as everything.

To admit otherwise
would mean admitting she's
dumb,
weak,
useless.

Women aren't useless.
Often tougher than men.
Many men, to be specific.
But they love to gnaw on issues.

As if worry made her wise.
But there's nothing sharp in circling the drain.
Just chewing what ain't there,
working herself up for the thrill of it.
That's not depth.
That's lunacy.

That's the difference between the sexes.
Women want the conflict
that is easily resolved.
Men want the conflict
that creates great art.

Women don't see it like men.
When asked if they could,
they backpedal boldly:
"Yes, I could do it...
but only if this and that was in place for me.
Or if I had this or that...
but I don't.
Not my fault."

Fathom the fool, they will not.
I've explained it all now.
So treat her that way.
And fuck already.
Christ, how sex solves problems.

You still don't get it?!
She'll test you:
"You're so lucky youuu don't have to deal with this."
That's her being brave.

She wants you to admit
that what she does is harder,
that it has more value.
To see her suffer
means you suffer with her.

She wants a mutual moment to toil.
To be seen, not solved.

So join her wallow.
Offer the recognition,
hold the solution.
It doesn't have to make sense.
It never did.

That's the conflict she clings to.
That's the strife she survives on.

Doing everything right
doesn't mean you're owed a damn thing.

Still, The Heart Has A Chance

Tied up in the insanity of loss.
My mind blanks,
and it feels like the only sense of reason.

The deep yearning,
the unexpected nature of her remains—
dark, darker than a purple sky.
And still, there seems to be nothing.

How muddled the mind becomes
when emotions reign.
Strange and aberrant,
the guarded heart is a defeatist.

Only when the fear of possibility strikes
do we pause for love.
The rarity of such a thing is frightening,
but to think it never exists is worse.
You feel it when you're not ready —
imperfection and grace, mixed together,
as a car whooshes past.

Stunned by a headlight,
the heart is reminded to take a chance.

Love is something we blindly believe in.
When the pieces fit,
connected with ease,
picture-perfect smiles held in place.
Time stands still.

But the mind is calculated—
complex, obstructive.
A bead of doubt bounces back and forth.
With great speed it takes over.
No longer taken by love.
Still, the heart has a chance.

There is nothing more miserable than wondering.
Moments of the past return,
former boundaries abruptly abandoned.

Last year's mistake becomes last night's mistake.

Upon the mounting pressure,
the only choice is to be alone.

Alone, when you could be together.
The hardest part.
Stupid and tortuous,
all because of love.

But endings weren't made for us.
We have now,
and what will be.

As our crossed paths merge
into forever memories,
when I can't help but be taken
by the way you look tonight
and every night hereafter.

And so I wait.
I wait for her.
She is my only one.
Because I know—
my heart has a chance.

Each generation seeks relevance,
yet meaning bends into bias.

Ignorance shadows their eyes,
and former greatness slips into silence.

Scarecrows Wear the Crown

All history is a romance,
a spool spun of individuality,
a sweater worn for every season.

If community is so strong,
why were kings assassinated?
Commercialization, commodification—
the purity of the vibe
rewired into profit.

Are there still authentic corners?
Places where the heart beguiles the buck,
where true artists sit alone,
alive and unwell,
still fighting the fight.
Or has the last great artist gone extinct?

Perhaps the opportunist is crowned instead:
a scarecrow full of straw,
stuffed with slogans,
manufactured for attention,
posed for crows,
still sucking.

Maybe the pace of culture is to blame:
everyone chasing the present moment,
obedience packaged as imperative.

I wouldn't know.
I'm too busy with my own art.
NYC keeps me sharp and depressed,
a perfect mix
of smut and inspiration.

I am my own experience.

But maybe I'm too smart.
I've studied, read too much.
I live knowing too much.
I've ruined life—
as you know it.

Strain

A result
may not
answer the question,
but it
reduces strain.

Vein of Addiction

I hate what I want,
but must feed what I need.

Like flesh sold by the minute,
we're bound to the same scheme.
We give up what's sacred,
spending what's left of our mercy.

This surrender turns us to nothing,
even when framed as right,
lying as we rot through it.

Belly up. Bladed. Broken.
A pool of blood at our feet.
We swim in the sea of red.
And we say it's worth it.

Veins shiver beneath whispers,
a secret life behind a smile.

Sanity frays,
one fix closer.
Don't break.
Come close.
Stay bound.
Don't breach what clutches you.
It never goes away anyway.

Withdrawal is hard,
so you keep using—
even if it costs everything,
even if it leaves you numb.

Until it's gone.
Until it turns.
Until it subsides.

Safe and Alone

I spent the entire day alone.
There were parties I could have gone to,
but I didn't want to be around anyone.

I felt anxious today —
more so than usual.

I lay down on my bed
and gazed up at the ceiling.
I had to practice breathing,
its rhythm disturbed
by the distraction of my thoughts.

I thought about myself.
I thought about the things I wanted to accomplish.
I thought of times I wasted,
of money I foolishly spent.
I thought of my sister.
I thought of my mother.
I thought of my ex-girlfriend.
I thought about it all too much,
until I became weary
and uncomfortable.

It must have been
one of the first nice days of spring.
I could tell through my shades.
I felt guilty for wanting to go outside,
guilty for wanting to see the sunset.
I felt I didn't deserve it.
I felt like I had failed the day.

The worst part about today
was no one knew I was this low.
On other days, when I felt this way,
I'd call a friend.
I'd read a book.
I'd play music and close my eyes.
I'd do yoga.

I'd do anything —
anything to derail attention
from my melancholy.

But today I let it take over.
I picked up my phone,
then put it down.
I didn't want to bother them.
I didn't want to ruin their day.
I didn't want to ruin their sunset.

I didn't know how to manage my melancholy.
That happens from time to time.
It's natural to feel that way.
Unlike happiness,
sadness is ready and willing.

So I remained alone.
It was the only way I felt safe.

And I wish sometimes
I didn't feel this way about myself.
As if ambition worked against me,
as if every success was outdated.

I know if you asked my friends,
they'd say I was a swell guy.
I guess I can be sometimes.
I guess I was just a few days ago.

How frustrating it is —
the past can feel so removed from today.

But the mind is a mysterious organ.
Sometimes I think mine obsesses
over past flaws committed.
I suppose anyone can forget
their own greatness.
It's hard to remember sometimes.

I know I'm not the only one.
There are others who woke up today
and felt the same.
Others will feel this way tomorrow.
There's no way of knowing
how any day will go.

It's supposed to be sunny again tomorrow.
And hell, just thinking of tomorrow
is already making today more tolerable.

I might as well sleep on all this
after I finish this poem.
Maybe I'll have a better crack at it
when I wake.

I'm feeling optimistic.
How about you?

The Steam Along Christie Street

We had just left the first bar,
and I was beginning to let myself go.
The humidity of August clung to me—
sweat mixing with gin,
with neon,
with the noise of another Saturday.

The anticipation of the night grew.
Strangers passed like shadows,
faces glowing,
half-heard voices calling my name—
or maybe they didn't.

The streets steamed,
tar-born fog rising in waves.
I stepped into it,
not caring what would happen,
fearless of what might,
fearful of what might not.

Glass on wood.
A speaker groaning.
A hand on my shoulder.
Laughter—too loud.
A kiss, maybe.
A stumble.
The floor tilting.
The night breaking apart
before it could land.

I was tired as sin,
but I didn't ask for forgiveness.
I granted myself salvation
when memory faded to black.

And still I walked,
carried by the blur,
by the heat,
by the city's senses.
Along Christie Street,
where steam turns into dread.

I, the Writer

Society looks to us
to fulfill a need—
a persona to make sense of things,
a voice both against
and for hypocrisy itself.
To be the truth.

The rock star is the rock star.
His antics—
pardoned,
because he is the person,
we wish we were meant to be..

I guess.
I'm the writer.

And though I self-loathe,
fear insignificance,
and fail to curb my anxiety,
I'm the writer.

I write for others
because they cannot.
I say what they want,
but don't.

I feel the uncertainty
of every word I place.
I feel the weight
of every critical reaction.

But I do it for the people
in lonely places,
who need something to read
to help them understand
what it all means.

That they are not alone.

That good days—
although limited—
outweigh the days
of clouded distortion,
bleak failure,
and moments not worth remembering.

For that,
I am the writer.

For that,
I write for you.

And perhaps,
I write for myself.

The Golden Armadillo

You do these things
with the intent of them being transactional.

That you'll be praised for it.
That you'll be raised for it.
That it will be the inner scope of all
the rush,
the feeling,
the excitement of being.

I think people call it purpose.
But it doesn't turn out that way.
The money piles.
The problems suck each cent dry.
The envy spreads like a plague.
Everyone wants something from you.
Nobody wants to give you anything other than
cheap words,
cheap shots,
cheap meaning.

And it all becomes a domicile of domestication,
advertised beside a roadside sign
asking about your devotion to Jesus.

Then the gears in your mind begin to turn:
Have you caught up?
Should you worry?
Will that worry compel you to take on more?
And is *more* really better?

It won't be.
It never was.
It never will be.

Rarely are we remembered,
but we act as though everyone is our spectator,
lurking, watching,
as if we'll be their model.

Everyone feeds off the thought
that they are being noticed,
even though they'll never know.
We live in an illusion
of fame, prestige, and abundance.

But we aren't models.
We're too fat,
too gullible,
too spread.

How can anyone work on their depth
when it doesn't fit
within the smorgasbord of surface-based appetizers?

We bury it beneath the faux representation of things,
stuff,
people,
impressions,
and the whole grab bag of society's utter bullshit.

A nation of gimmicks and critics.
All framed as progress,
but it's a trend in the end.

But we must eat.
And when we eat, we want to eat better.
And when it gets better,
we want what's well.

And that's when we start to transform.
Into something armored.
Calloused.
Preserved by pain.

That's when we become the Golden Armadillo.

But enlightenment has never come
from anything unwritten,
unproduced,
or unpainted.

The digital spheres have taken over that.
The ramifications of
sound,
light,
views—
mingled with the ever-effervescent trap of
marketing,
positioning,
entrapment.

Sadly,
the honest boy waits to see clearly
but the canvas was never blank.

It was always scripted:
the way it should be.
Must be.
Could only be.

And security appears,
not as salvation,
but as survival.

Its back is tough.
Its body hidden.
Its smile forced.

His partner.
His baby.
Clenches that smile with jagged teeth,
a performance of pain
beguiled by the performative monster of mediocrity.

To be in the race
with the counterparts next door,
down the road,
across the state,
in the country,
within the world.

All of whom they never cross paths with.

While we spit in the eye
of someone who actually comes close to touching us.
Instead, we champion anger in their place.
Bitter they let the world do it to them
before they could do it back.

But we stroke our golden shell.
Filling our days with lots of cluttered conversations
about celebrations that others have or haven't done—
but never about what they should be doing.

The keepsakes of our *blah, blah, blah*
don't come from the sound of our fury.

No.

They come from the superficial selections
of what we emulate, imitate,
and remonstrate as our own originality.

Through stern sincerity,
the liver of our lives forgets to filter the hogwash.
The boar reminisces about a regret it boasts
as if it happened.
And we oink when we're told to.
We squeal with unoriginality.

I could.
I might.
If only...oink.

The phrases that riddle our incessant being
skirting the very ounce of originality
that might've flourished.

We wish to be hung to dry
as a butcher gives the gift of death
to the devil in the swine.

Even with these notions,
we swoon from the sidelines,
edging toward the mainstream.

Thinking that we must be liked.

But reputation is a snake we watch,
and the genie of our soul
has always granted one wish: Validation.

"I matter, you know."

We pounce with the prediction
that we could be more.

More for whom?

Who knows.

How miserable our lives become
when we wish to see them as valid to others.

Maybe I don't get it.
You might say I have it wrong.
Maybe that's so.
Still, I unravel along the way.
Or maybe you'll think more clearly.
Maybe you think he's as right as any of us.

Outside praise does not refine us
unless it was always intended so.
That damn shell—how it protects us.
But it doesn't in the end;
it's just heavy,
delicate,
and calculated.

Forcing itself.
Involved for the sake of involving.

As tough as the bare back
of our bony shell,
we scratch at it
until we convince ourselves it's smooth.

But it isn't.
It's carnivorous.
It's ancient.
It's sacred.

It's a reminder we refuse to see.

So we remain—
not caged,
but enclosed within our own armor,
our own gilded tomb.

Along the Peppercorn Road

Choice in the matter
shifts along the peppercorn road.

Dotted and dashed
by the specks of lofty ideals—
turned dry by the gravel,
grinding against
who we knew ourselves to be.

Pleasure subsides
the moment we yearn
for something more.

But what?

What was essential
turns temporary—
as direct an assault
as we wish for,
as we no longer need.

Even desire
has an obstructed view.
The gravy is found
in abstractions.

Until it becomes clear
it is arbitrary—
no meaning,
until we decide
nothing else matters.

The sting of our spontaneity
is never spontaneous,
laced backwards.
It was only through
the derision of time—
a catacomb of experience,
bursting with anger—
and it must be ours then.
We refuse nothing.

There's safety in the unresolved;
once you solve it,
what's left to handle?

Drama is a drug.
I'm hooked.

No Equilibrium

In life
there is no equilibrium.
Some success,
more failure.

Everything in-between
transactional.
It's either it,
or what of it.

There's evidence to report,
or potential to qualify.

When offering nothing
but your own misunderstanding
churns like steel teeth,
tearing away at
a story,
a song,
a memory.

And in the wake of those moments,
the wonder becomes a whirl,
a spinning sensation of joy—
Because discovery
is the disjointed
nature of alignment.

It's only on the creator,
who finds
whatever it is,
whatever it could be,
whatever was the it
they didn't know
in the first place.

Cheers, Night

To blue skies that blind back.

To strangers who become friends,
and friends who become strangers.

To misfortunate misfits,
drinking blissful beers
over soggy coasters.

To queens who howl at the moon,
while princes watch
in patient admiration.

To shattered feet,
chance meets,
and unexpected 3 a.m. strolls.

To the night.
To the next night.
To the light that takes this night.
To every night.
To the night.

Just like wind,
people blow you away.

Fight

I've reached a time where I don't have to,
but security feels foreign.
Even the smallest obstacle sets me off.

I fight for reasons unknown to others—
my friends,
my girlfriend,
my boss,
my family.

The aggression builds.
It terrorizes my mind.
At times it makes me cry—
a volcano mounting,
red syrup oozing from my tear ducts.

A lit match dazzles in front of me.
All I have to do is blow it out.
But I watch it.
The blackened wick grows,
the feud falls,
and I wait for the moment
the last light lives.

There is serenity in darkness.
It is wild.

The whole time I am afraid to be exposed.
No one even knows it happened.
They smile.
I smile back.

Hidden behind the times
when fighting was the only option—
I revert.

Sometimes it's easier
to be the person you used to be.

I love money,
but hate providing.
I love drinking,
but hate the hangover.
I love women,
but hate the heartbreak.

Rich Girls

Rich girls don't worry about rent.

"How do you pay rent?"
"I don't."
"Who does?"
"My grandparents."

They putter through the week,
babysitting gigs turned into paid friendships.
Master's degrees drift into one-week trips
to France, Spain, Maui.
A thesis swallowed with matcha at brunch—
"I guess it's my passion.
I don't even know if it's worth it."

How ironic is the value of a rich girl?

Rich girls marry rich boys.
Those boys obsess over their rich girls.
The rich girls love it,
hate it,
live with it.

But rich girls like guys like me.
Rough-and-tumble types.
The kind who's fine if they're there,
fine if they're not.
They always want to be wanted.
They can't stand my disconnect.

"Why are you like this?
Every other guy falls over me!"
I shrug.
"It's okay, baby. Come here."
I kiss her forehead,
the spot of resolve—
just like her daddy used to do.

But what I think is much different.
'Cause when they're here, I lose sleep—
entertaining someone whose life

is built on instant entertainment,
reaction, stimulation,
while they offer very little.

A curated saga, dealt with in an instant
or dragged out whenever convenient.
How pathetic to create melodrama
for the happenstance of killing time.

And when they're gone,
I write about them.
Like now.
Because they fascinate me in a different way.
Not lust exactly—
sure, we fuck.
Rich girls are more open sexually,
maybe liberated by the fact
that if mistakes occur,
they can be solved.
"No babies for me yet."
On that, we agree.

What draws me to rich girls is something else—
their unusual excuse to live.
No true desire beyond being aloof.
They don't build. They just do.
Maneuvering through social scenes,
never finding what they're looking for.
How could they?
They were always given whatever they wanted.

Security is a highway with painted lines.
Survival is potholes, rubble, broken ground.
Rich girls like the idea of survival
but prefer the comforts of smooth pavement.
They stay bound to the lifestyle they despise,
kicking and screaming through their joyride.

They wish they could be miserable—
carry some trauma.
Something to define them.

But humanity isn't what confuses them.
It's that they've never had to face it.
They never will.
They wouldn't know how to bear it.
But I do.
And they want what they can't have.
And that's exactly what they can't get:
a raw guy to mold.
Unlike their trappings,
I stay free.

Yet sometimes, sparks.
Oddball moments—
sitting naked on a couch,
a bowl of M&Ms microwaved hot,
watching a Picasso documentary.

That's when rich girls are ruined.
Because all the money in the world
can't make them poor.
They'd never bend over backwards for you—
but in rare moments, they do.
And in those moments, they see what it's like.

But still—
it costs to be free.

If relevance is all we see,
we forget where it came from.

No regrets.
Just memories, moments, and maybes.

Anatomy of Doubt

A solitary man
allows himself to think.
Uncertainty intoxicates his soul.

He builds an ecosystem
of chaos and distraction—
threads left loose.

Pressures rise
toward the inevitable end—
superfluous in retrospect,
yet supremely built
on infatuation,
on fear,
on the loneliness
of what he might reveal
or what he might never name.

Virtue of Risk

The consequence of being safe
is staying safe.
And that never aligns
with risk.

Risk is the only virtue
worth its vice.

Sometimes looking like hell is a good thing.

Privacy Notice

The guy told me his license plate was from Pennsylvania.
I said, "You live in Pennsylvania?"
He goes, "No, I live in Connecticut."
"Then why the different plate?"
"Privacy," he said.
"Cops don't stop out-of-state plates."

I thought,
What an asshole.

What privacy does he need?
What secrets is he safeguarding?
What grand gesture warrants this cloak of invisibility?

Nobody wants to know you.
Nobody's trying to get into your business.
Why would they?

What have you done that's so magnificent?
What burden do you carry
that deserves protection from the eyes of the world?

Does the economic infrastructure
of the country reside in your hands?
You can barely pay for gas.

But sure,
switch the license plates,
scheme for privacy,
plot your anonymity.

What a great use of time.
All in the name of privacy.

Privacy,
the soliloquy of silence
for someone desperate to be heard.

They build stories of duress
just to explain their evasions,
exposing their own schemes
to anyone dumb enough to listen.

Anyone willing to hear.
Anyone who might care.
Anyone who might validate the struggle
of the great privacy warrior.

If you want privacy,
why aren't you in a dark room,
cornered by piss bottles,
collected weekly by a man who doesn't give a shit?

Send letters by foot.
No stamps.
Meet people in person.
No phones.
Use cash.
No credit cards.
Starve.
No drive-thru
at midnight with a burger, fries, and a shake.

Cameras everywhere.
Receipts tied to your name.
If they want to find you, they will.

There is no privacy.
None.

And the ones who try hardest to preserve it
are often the most noticed.

While the rest of us,
those who bare our souls,
those who try to write something decent,
we're told to shut up.

Too busy,
too noisy,
listening to some guy
brag about bucking the system,

Pennsylvania plates on his Silverado.
But he lives in Connecticut.

Doctors Are Not Storytellers

I call doctors
the most prolific reciters of regurgitation.

They haven't discovered anything.
They just say what's already known,
already around—
but take it as theirs.

They can't perceive my role;
they were taught it wasn't possible.
But I just write better.

Doctors are not storytellers.
They are reporters.

They report on the natural phenomena of biology—
what was there before them,
what will be there with them,
what will be there after.

Slow to start,
quick to snatch glory—
it's at an all-time high with my physicians.
A way to justify what they studied,
defined by the parameters of their degree.

The one note they clutch,
even though credibility fails
the moment it's handed to them.

They lose drive
because they've used it up—
just to say the potential is theirs.

But few resist reluctance.
Only those become gods among the scalpel.
Most cut themselves off early on.

They'd rather be told they could
than show they did.

That's my reason, I suppose:
to make them appear smart.

Line by line,
I clean up the garbage,
turning their words into miracles.
People see them as genius,
and me—
they'll never know.
Because they wouldn't believe it otherwise.

Fifteen years, five hundred publications,
and all I get—
"a good organizer."

They're told, "How smart you are to write this."
And what is smart, anyhow,
other than permission from others—
most times like-minded,
nodding within invisible hierarchies.

It's not the accolade that sorrows me,
it's the perception that's granted,
loosely wired to their names on a manuscript,
a declaration without creation.

No—what angers me is the misuse of terms.
They are not genius.
Genius doesn't wait for credit.
Genius doesn't cling to titles.
Genius doesn't stop at the boundaries of a degree.

But genius never stops.
He's too busy with the next project,
the next paper,
the bleak attempt to create art.

Meaning comes from conflict—
the true test of genius.
But there aren't any geniuses.
It's a guise we quickly denote.

So when you write a paper about science,
stick to the study—
not yourself.

Balloons for Banality

Bland accolades of grandeur
continue to be thrown
for the modest notions
of mediocrity.

What an absence of humanity,
souls reduced to a gimmick.

And for what?
An action.
A reaction.
A machination for sport.

A guy sits on the subway
with a microphone,
and suddenly
he's someone we must listen to.
"I agree."
"I don't agree."
The ooh and ahh of dullness.

We see the world as meaningful
when we are young—
that we'll have impact,
that we'll contribute.

We think what's now
must mean more
than what came before.
So we grasp at the present,
straws drawn in frantic speed.

"It must mean something!"
"It's different because it's me."
"It's our time."

But later we see
we've done very little.
Wasted opportunity,
requiring solitude,
craving acceptance

from those who've never accepted themselves.

And then we tire of the hunt.
We bleed at first—
unnoticed.
Then it drains us dry.
We walk with little life left.

We turn to escapes.
We drink.
We drug.
We cheat.
We do all the things
we swore we wouldn't.

And we do them with vindication—
as if the whispers of morning
told us we had no chance.

Still, we act the part.
Smile on command.
Agreeable,
unrecognizable
to our former selves.

Convincing ourselves,
convincing others,
that what we do
is what they should do.

The herd rumbles
louder than any buffalo stampede.
The divide between dreamers and doers
narrows to nothing.

"Slim chance," they say.

How cruel it becomes
when the visions of yesterday
become the vanished dreams of today.

Like the rock with no rough edges.
Like the arrow with no head.
Like the gun with no bullets.

The house of cards collapses.
One missing piece
and our innards spill—
splat on the table,
blood drying
before it pools.

Because it's the biggest issue we face:
the concept of surrender.
And we dress it up as victory.
That's the worst place to be—
where you applaud your own fear,
failure dressed as surrender,
applause arriving
as slow acceptance.

Our color may shine,
but it dries like paint.
It fades with the season.
We're lucky
to ever get a fresh coat.

Promise turns to presence
faster than it should.
Instead of resisting,
we settle into default.

Once a string held our balloon,
but we're afraid to rise—
afraid we haven't amounted to enough.
So we ache alone—
unsure,
unable,
unreal.

And we can’t help
but feel relieved—
the saddest relief,
no longer required,
no longer breathing
in the spectacle.

We wait for the pin.
One puncture.
Air gone.
Finally.

The balloons of banality
drift off,
empty,
gone.

Fail valiantly, with laughter and humility,
so the sky burns red with rage
and turns black with wonder.

Her voice was a feather
that caught the wind
in just the right way
and carried on forever.

Among, But Not Of

I've always felt
as though I'm observing.

Observing people,
places,
interactions—
their concerns,
their elations,
their desires.

Always observing.

The difficult part
is that I always feel out of place,
even when welcomed
with open arms.

I'm not steady,
so I'd rather watch.
I find it more interesting.

And I wonder—
can I ever fit in?

Friction is why fire flames.

Sweetleaf

I saw my best self
in her brown eyes.
The way I always hoped
to be seen.

I held her hand differently after that.
Squeezed lightly.
As if to say
we could hold each other up.

Our first kiss wasn't a trick.
Not a game,
not a fling,
not desperation.

It was belief.
A stumble toward trust.

First dates don't usually give you that.

But sometimes
the strike hits,
sparks crack,
fire runs through you,
and the past caves in.

Be ready when it happens.
Forever doesn't wait around.

You can be sober
but still get drunk.

Combat congenial ignorance
with subtle genius.

Cheap Chopsticks

The mind of a woman
is her predicament—
fickle as cheap chopsticks,
breaking under her own trap.

She seeks stability inside,
yet craves chaos outside.

Sensitive, because she is caught.
Alluring, because she cannot escape.
Darkly beautiful, because mystery always bites back.

Seasons in a Bowl

It's a first date.

The Russian girl is stunning.
But I notice the bowl of rice
more than her,
sitting between us.
The rice steams,
but the beads,
from afar,
look like cold flakes of snow,
forged into a sloping bowl—
grey, shiny, content.

And the rice reminds me
of winters in Maine—
a day trip taken
with a college friend
who broke his collarbone.
The ski patrol came,
sledded us down to the base,
slung him up.
I drove us home.
That year,
the season
was cut short.

I always think about that—
or any season
where we miss out,
where something else—
even injury—
takes precedence.

And I think about this woman across from me,
and how I won't miss our season.
Who knows where it'll go,
how dubious our incantation is
when we see through inhibitions.

She asks me what my life motto is.
I tell her it's *commit first, convince later.*
She likes that.
She thinks about all the times
she didn't commit.

And then she says,
"Want some rice?"

And I say,
"No need to convince me."

The Agony of the Ordinary

I want to be around people who are evil.
Not the kind who are malicious—no.
But the ones who are interesting.

Often the speed of life slows
to a pale dullness.
A safety net of latticework,
the cage of conformity.
Fed scraps—
hungry for conventionality.

They say they want *something*,
but what extraordinary thing have they brought?

Nothing, usually.
False promise.
Not even a lie.
At least a lie excites.
But the tech company,
the accounting firm,
the dogshit carousel of interest rates—
that isn't astonishing.

Yet you beg for someone to excite you.
But you're not exciting.

Working for Microsoft? Not exciting.
Those leopard-print leggings Instagram sold you? Not exciting.
That tattoo you got in Costa Rica fifteen years ago? Not exciting.

What's exciting is intrigue.
Projects protect it.
Sitting at the damn keyboard,
spilling your guts before they rot.
Show us.
Don't tell us.
Creations rarely give answers,
but at least they hold a reason.

Burn a hole through our brains.

Women will say they want a guy
who stands out,
but often he falls short—
just like them,
riding the pine of potential,
endless conversations about
what could be done
if they really wanted to.

Women prepare for disposal—
just as the work is done,
at the time he most needs her.
When his anguish weakens,
she feels smaller than the work.

So she leaves.

She finds someone safer,
back to the poppy patch of potential.
Until she finds a loser who never fulfills his dream.
Then—oops. A kid. A dog. A house.
Now nothing else can be done.

And somehow that's different?

How far can one laugh take us,
when it pushes further away,
our inner betrayal
basking in its own victory.

Shucks.
Settled.
Saved from obscurity.
The hollow dream,
a leaking faucet left to drip—
existence bartered,
inevitable steps repeated.

How obedient one becomes
when they realize their rarity is gone.

Rather than confess,
they try to change us into them,
to preserve who they've become,
and kill those who once were them.
So some of us revolt.
When there's no voice, no edgewise escape.
When you can't convince them of your way of life,
there's nothing left but to write.

At least then,
you've killed one dragon.
A quiet victory
among their boredom.

They will be heard. They demand it.
They like the sound of their own voices,
though silence would explain it all.
Spewed into nothingness,
routine lives they latch onto.
Rushing. Exhausted.
Showcasing devotion—
birthday parties,
days at the zoo,
holiday cookies in plastic wrap—
perfect lives performed in fluorescent light.

No room to sit, or sleep, or say anything.
A shattering sound imposed on others.
As if it were ever right
to walk the pathway to ordinary.

"An impressive decision we've made."

Is it?
I'm not so sure.

Ordinary is agony.

Living in limbo leaves you without leverage.

Plastic Bags on Branches

The goods weigh us down—
stable, unstable,
ready to break without notice.

We add more.
We take more.
We see less.

The start is flat,
the recent peaks—
until it all compacts.

Pulled by our handle,
the elastic snaps.
Everything gone,
sprawled on the sidewalk—
and it's the best feeling we've ever had.

The pressure snaps,
the rising inferiority gone.
The air picks us up.

Flying, we wrap around a branch—
twisted, mangled,
our fibers stretched.

The branch waits to let go,
just as we did—
the same way before.

Until we're free to fly,
no strings attached.

Find your eternal escape
beyond the ordinary.

I don't know anything—
that I know for sure.

The Burning Eclipse

Smokers are risk takers.
They light up,
knowing with every puff
they get closer to death.

Maybe they've got it all figured out—
the late-night booze,
the magenta bruises under their eyes,
the phantoms of nightlife,
the congregation
around a dying flame.

Rush and pageantry.

Life could never feel so low,
so great,
so exciting.

Maybe the smoker
has it all figured out.
I wish I did.
I wish anyone did.

Sandstorms in Our Mind

Reputation is a phantom in the sand—
a ghost we become from birth.

How quick we dwindle,
worshipping the dune gobbler—
aiming at an imaginary target,
closing in on us.

We believe the illusion,
all for vanity's pursuit.
Seeping backward from suffering,
heeding fast from existence,
before being criticized
and torn by the crowd's fangs.

But we take it.
Demoralized by some spittoon figure—
better mutilated in flesh
than entombed in the mind.

Trauma cements our chaos—
an immobile, safe face,
a sandcastle that never meets the sea.

Responsibility strikes a pose;
we pass the buck—
to others in orbit,
to artificial intelligence,
our resolute scapegoat.

Hasn't it always been
someone else to blame?
If that were true,
why do we still idolize?

"Not us, no way."

Why recoil, again and again,
from the phantom in the sand?
We stray from the truth
because of the monster.

Inside, we are bursting.
Outside—pale as the ghost—
a blank canvas
that stays blank.
No colors to finger paint.
If we did,
our hands would only be full of sand.

More mood.
Less moody.

Nothing Wasted

Don't litter the mind.
Don't squander the illusions
you're trying to turn into realities.

Once, innovation was fantasy.
The fool who dared became the flyer.
Wild men and women believed in wings.

Don't litter the wish.
Don't discard the dream—
the force that demands to explore.

The road is full of cracks
to the careful eye.
Details deepen
through attention.

Follow them
straight into the rusted teeth of destiny.

A Link Through a Loophole

Some of us have links;
most have loopholes.

Some people become doctors
because their families own the hospitals.
Others claw into fields
through grunt work,
until that work shines like a jewel in their eyes—
then it's ripped from ours
before we even lose sight of it.
And we sit there,
digging for another loophole.

The linked ones never sweat.
Their résumés are stitched in gold
before they even write a word.
They walk into offices,
call it fate—
when really, it's a bloodline bribe.
Their mistakes are forgiven,
their incompetence
just called "potential."

The loophole crowd?
We build ladders from broken planks.
Our links are late nights,
side hustles,
cheap rent in rat-bitten basements.
We survive on duct tape and caffeine,
on maybe next year,
on if-I'm-lucky.

The linked ones think struggle
is choosing between caviar and lobster
at the company retreat.
The loophole crew thinks struggle
is a light bill due Friday
and a boss who says
"Be grateful you're even here."

The thinkers sit high in towers,
worrying about their words—
what sounds ignorant,
what might fracture a reputation—
as if reputation itself
weren't just another hand-me-down.

Meanwhile, the loophole finders
get called reckless,
called desperate,
called fools.
But we keep moving—
through cracks,
through back doors,
through the spaces
where links can't reach.

And sometimes,
when you go through enough loopholes,
you become the link.
Because loopholes may not last forever,
but they're ours.

And that's enough.

We never needed permission.

Dogshit Stew

We've created more problems
trying to solve solutions
than to solve actual problems—
all in the name of one
imposing their ideals
as the better way of handling things.

If it worked then,
why not now?
"Times are different."
"That's the old way."
"It's not new."
Excuses. All of them.

The truth?
We're just bored.

We think our take matters.
We don't think, craft, or mull over thoughts.
We just say what we say
for the sake of sport and entertainment.

We crave the attention
that comes from frivolous accolades of peers.
We think we have to
keep up with our contemporaries.

We obsess over a fallout
that hasn't dropped.
We invent disasters
to parade our solutions,
all in the name of being a savior.

All the while avoiding
the real problem—us:
who we are,
who we become in the process.

Adamant still,
shouting independence.
But all it is—

faux.
feign.
thump.

A pocket full of posers—
all fall down.
Not strong,
not courageous,
not bold.
Meek, moody,
desperate for release.

Folding the moment we're told what to do.

Drowning in dogshit stew—
gasoline poured in,
stewed to burn,
blown up,
and somehow bailed out
for our indulgence in ignorance.

We clap it away.
We forgive ourselves.
We matter, we say—
but we don't.

We're just products—
technology's grip on the psyche,
corporate brainwash,
loser culture dressed as influence,
spaghetti Sundays,
craft lager,
gender reveals,
crypto coins,
Instagram reels,
and a cold brew from Dunkin'.

All the smut we buy into—
and if nothing else,
we'll find a problem there too.

Talking Headless Horsemen

Moral judgment now rests
on a single assessment:
relevancy.

And with it,
the death of belief.

Belief in God—
once final, undone,
pitched like a used car salesman's script.

Belief in self—
rebellion shrunk to convention,
selfhood dimmed to sameness.

Belief in society—
community dressed as commodity,
togetherness staged as aesthetic.

Technology creeps in
as the ultimate replacement.
It exchanges pleasure for power,
touting control
under the rule of committees.
They dictate how, why, and when we act—
life reduced to insinuations.

All of this grows
from a hunger for permission.
We ache to be told what to do.
Not desire dictating permission—
but permission dictating desire.

But relevance is not art.
Creation takes conflict—
not violent,
but an inner fight.

Even if solitude requires time to become,
it's worth the wait.
Pace is our priority.

Only patience sets us free.

Otherwise,
lost souls are erased.
Washed away
in the cheap heat of visibility.

There's urgency for now—
even though truth
demands silence,
demands seasons.

But why so impatient?
For proof of existence itself?
To be seen as we've always existed?

You've never thought so deeply on this—
until now.

Because your life has turned—
convenient, metric-based, materialistic.

Even health gets shortcut—
a pill for performance,
not for life.
Bodies sculpted for show,
not strength.

And so you are told:
This is what relevance looks like.
What you should look like.
Talk like.
Think like.
Be like.

Until the talking head collapses.
The horsemen gallop.
A nation rots in its chant.

And when all are forced to think alike,
the outlier is always shot—
or, in the end,
he kills himself.

Greatness offends the mediocre.
So we muzzle it—
unless it peeks through the keyhole of empathy.

Bubbles and Birthdays

The pink flamingo jostled
under the willow tree in Brooklyn.

Little boys and girls lined up straight
as the bubble machine spun and wiggled orbs.

Each one nearly popped
as they passed through children's faces.
Baguettes and brie baked on the picnic table.
Mothers and fathers anticipated,
searching for a way
to make this birthday—
a great birthday.

I watched from a short distance.
The declivity of the grassy hill
formed a small amphitheater around their scene.

The bubbles floated past me.
Every so often I dodged,
just as the piñata swerved past
the three-year-old's attack.

The stick was taller
than even the tallest child.

The parade of children clamored
for the candy center.
And as the final smash split the flamingo,
the jewels of sugar dispersed.

Bubbles popped in faces
and tangled in hair.

One bubble drifted toward me,
slower than the others,
suspended
as if daring me to blow.

But it did not want to fly away.
It landed next to me,
holding on to the greenest blade
before bursting.

I smiled and thought—
until the next piñata,
until the next bubble,
until the next birthday.

And So Are We

There's a narrow stop in Dumbo,
the hub that looks up to the Brooklyn Bridge.
Just around the corner from the carousel,
outside the cobblestone streets.

It's nearing sunset.
Late-shift workers mingle with tourists—
those from Battery Park or Beijing,
scattered like polished ladybugs,
vying for a seat on the ferry.

Soon the clerk scans tickets.
A bum rush to the top deck—
limited seating, limited views,
limited experiences.
The rookies want to take it all in.
The veterans just want to sleep.

Even the beaten-down banker knows the times.
The seamstress from Astoria only wants home.
A waitress thinks about her new lover
just off Wall Street.

The ferry is a relic of adventure,
a fleeting what-if of being lost at sea.
But these citizens rush to sit,
to scroll phones, swipe left,
gasp at some dancing video,
read one sentence of an article
and call it good enough,
comment with an emoji,
adding to the juggernaut of new-age media.

Then the horn blows—
the ferry cuts water
like a knife through watermelon,
rind grinding, juice spilling.

We push forward through the turmoil of land
into the abyss of the river.
Rats on cement watch us go by.

Domino Park's old bones,
the sugar factory turned to a gym,
the taco seller waves—
all day, every day,
free marketing like the nitwit clock
that's right twice,
though somehow hands
always move faster than time.

And the girl I'm with—
I'm unsure if she'll last.
Our lives muddle the romance.
All love ruins itself
by trying to figure it out.
But the ferry doesn't think,
the water rises the same way
it always does.

A black man asks what building is ahead.
"The Empire State," I answer.
An easy one, but nice to know.
Fourteen years of rent
buys the right to certainty.

The ferry bumps,
rain falls, drops slide from head to feet.
The wet everywhere—rigid, unyielding—
still, we move.
A translucent tube of fog,
one neon sign away from elsewhere.
But no—we reach 34th Street.
Most disembark.
Few go to Queens.
We do.
The switch snaps,

we leave the dock again.
All this under the careful supervision
of a captain—or a steerer
leaning on the navigation system of the day.

It's night now.
The rain stops.
Dull as seagulls,
time has passed the same for us
as for centuries before.
Seventy years if we're lucky,
but technology transcends—
like love,
something we think begins with us
but always lived before,
and will after.

The girl with dark hair—
maybe just another fading cascade.
Or maybe not.
We haven't decided.
For now the engine roars,
we sail on,
we kiss because
it's a nice thing to do on a boat.

The city lights spark old wonder.
It will never be as new as it is for us.
So we keep it that way.
She keeps me in her way.
I keep her in mine.

Astoria at last.
The ride is over.
And so are we.

Live now. Die later.
You will anyway.

Wild Raspberries

All we have are our stories.
Preserve them. Dress them in gold.
Tell them to anyone who will listen.
For stories are the raspberries of life.

It'll never be enough,
but better something than nothing.

With Plaster on Our Face

What a vacant life we live
when the soul is stripped
and sold back to us
in curated fragments.

Performance splashed
like an out-of-body tragedy,
the world's ugliness
reflected in faces we once admired—
the ones we hoped
could see us,
speak to us
in sight, sound, and grace.

But they don't.
They never did.

That's grief—
the kind that grinds your worth into dust,
spread thin across envy's face,
like plaster shaped by hands
no one remembers.

And yet grief, cruel as it is,
sometimes sets you free.

Perhaps even the most popular aesthetics
are meant to be opposed in time.
Value leaks through cracks,
peeks through the keyhole
of doors locked by the ruling class—
who stand inside like a clan,
deciding what gets seen
and what stays forgotten.

What's worth noting
isn't just the bruise of personal rejection—
it's the broader forewarning.

Culture always loops back.
Even rebellion gets sold,
reheated,
repackaged—
a revolution rented by the hour.

But there's another kind:
quieter, less adorned.
Earned.
Staggering through the storm
with no applause.
That's the one that lasts.

We won't be the first.
The streets have history.
We walk alongside names.
We become what has become before.

But don't be dismayed—
even failure leaves a story.
Many live their whole lives
without one.

But you and me—
we have ours.

And if you don't have one,
what's the point?

Jolted by Jizz

Sex isn't an elixir.
It's an eliminator.
Great men have lost greatness.
Strong women, their will.

Sex is escapism—
from wherever we were before.
We bear the weight of being
just to distract ourselves with lust.

No force dissolves the dream of self
like chasing validation through sex.
The painter swears by it.
The poet despises it.
The accountant depends on it.

It's not soul we want touched—
but flesh.
We use another's body to fill our own,
reduce theirs to pleasure,
reduce ours to proof.

And what a view.
The pink petals of a woman,
a journey to eternity.
The man's joystick just rumbles,
inside and out.

How dull is it to be him.
How dull to be human.

Once, we were impenetrable.
But we can't live without it.
The instinct.
The blood.
The hormones.
A pot of gold.

But gold is for fools.
And so are we for sex.
Still—hell, it feels good.

Doesn't it?

The seduction of sensation
pulls us from our courage.
The ego's last refuge—
our bodies, splayed for the taking.

Even the smartest,
the richest,
the dumbest—
we all fall prey
to the music of the body.

The voice speaks,
but we don't listen.
We just let it in.
Like someone else's misery.

Until we orgasm.
Our brains—
jolted by jizz.

And then clarity.
Like before.
Before we came.
Before the sex.
It's over now.

Until we get insecure,
call it horny,
and go another round.

Because if someone wants to fuck us—
surely it means something.
We think it does.
We pray it does.

But it's just the fusion.
Heat between bodies,
waiting for the bang.

But often,
the real explosion—
the one where you surprise yourself—
you miss it.

Because you'd rather get fucked
and ache
than withstand
and create.

But don't fret.
That's how most end up.
Far from what once turned them on,
and only closer
to someone
who left behind
something similar.

Just to be touched.

Nothing is as pivotal as the present—
until tomorrow comes.

Editorial Waste Land

One letter.
One letter—repeat.
One word.
One word—repeat.
One sentence.
One sentence—repeat.
One paragraph.
One paragraph—repeat.
One page.
One page—repeat.
One story.
One story—repeat.

Wasted.
Until nothing remains.

Rejection fuels the strength
to prove the world wrong.

It Lingers

Maybe I'm one of the last renegades.

I do the work.
I try to do it well.
I sit in my own sludge of denial,
wondering if I've got what it takes,
all the while knowing
how easy it would be to surrender.

But I can't surrender.
I can't stop writing—
what if the perfect sentence is out there?

What anguish I wouldn't wish on you:
the tide of my thoughts,
already old as they leave,
yet somehow, fresh ones enter.

So I scribe relentlessly,
horrified I will forget,
horrified I will remember.

The pendulum swings to and fro:
that it won't be good enough,
that there must be more to find.

All the while
I could turn away from the ordeal.
I'm told it doesn't matter.
"Why bother?"
"What are you getting out of it?"

More than they know.
More than I'll ever know.

Whatever little thing becomes ours,
even the faintest melody is noble.

Keep what is yours.
Fight the urge.
Don't numb yourself

and become the splatter
of the status quo.
There's plenty of spilt ink in the world.
Most of it has kissed a ring.

Those who aren't renegades—
deceptive, sour,
gone down the furlongs
of surrender's grasp.

Their spirits sold.
I'm unsure where you buy them.
I've only been gifted one.
No amount of equity could take it.
It's the only thing I know for sure
will be in the grave.

So move past taking.
Show us your make.
Build it so it's done well.
Do it. Do it. Do it anyway.

Minor details wear us down.
Meaning matters more than mistakes.
Don't get lost in simple conditioning.

Rarity isn't existence itself.
It's how you shape your pursuit.

Maybe you see self-discovery
as a gimmick,
a performance of life,
where academia, metrics, and philosophy collide,
clumsy as a toddler's first grasp.

So what.
Keep reaching.

Even when the proof is there,
others may refuse to look at it.
Still, when the renegade is ignored,
he knows it's there.

The renegade's revelry is a lonely one.
Evidence against the system
he broke—
and breaks again.

Hold on to that proof.
It's the only thing we've got.
No matter your burden,
it's not you that's fucked,
it's the refusal of the renegade.

Even cowboys were once heroes—
saints no longer raised by praise.

A path that left many men broken,
a burden that became curse,
then anguish,
then privilege.

Rugged independence
betrayed by the culture that birthed it,
scorned in the memory of bootstraps.

And we've forgotten the glory of pursuit.
For without pursuit,
there is no will.
And without will,
there is no swan song.

It lingers.
It will linger,
even for the last renegade.

Should we sell our soul
just to buy it back?

How to Handle It

The course of progress
trips on itself
because people can't listen,
won't read,
refuse to follow directions.

But sure. Make it all up.
By all means, do it your way.
Don't follow the proven directions.

Some half-flung method
you just stitched together
because it gives you authority—
a chance to rewrite the rules
without a single track record.

"I didn't understand."
Of course you didn't.
Not because it wasn't clear—
but because you never bothered to look.

"I thought you meant..."
No. You thought nothing.
You wanted your way—
ignoring what was already established.

"It's not the way I'd handle it."
The wheel was already built—just push it.
You were asked to turn the handle,
not critique its spin.

"I figured you wanted initiative."
No, I didn't ask you to figure out anything.
I wanted accuracy.
I wanted the job done.

"I'll just do it my way. You'll get it."
Thanks for the mess.
Thanks for ignoring fifteen years of refinement,
brick by brick,
so you could pretend your shortcut mattered.

No, your feelings don't get to break it.
No, your shortcuts don't get to erase it.
And no—
not even AI can bail you out.

The directions weren't unclear.
You were.

Next time—
read my fucking directions.

Fame

Success → Destr ction
Big Break → Destruction
Persevere → Dest u tion
Blunder → Des u ion
Build → De u on
Seek → D u n
Pursue → u

Your public face
is not your private priority.

Devotion

We consider devotion
earns us the gift of
reception,
recognition,
and regality.

So we marry.
We have kids.
We work twenty years.
And all of it—
we impress as a rite of passage,
through some magnified illusion of meaning.
But we don't need more of the ordinary.

We don't need devotion
to the conventions of society.
No.
They've had enough of
our time,
our grace,
our soul.

A graveyard screams with mediocrity—
and we visit it every so often
to remind ourselves
we aren't doing as bad as they did.
That we amounted to more.

But is it more?
Or is it the same rerun,
on again—
same plot,
same people—
just different faces,
fearing the inevitable regret of ordinariness.

I once saw a man with potential.
I now see a crowd full of shit.
It's devotion to the norm that plagued us,
like a dog leashed in a fenced backyard—
large, hilly,

free to explore,
but stuck in a corner,
where dirt mixes into mud.

The son of a bitch just
wishes to break free.
Like us,
again and again.
We'd do anything
to grasp the aliveness
we once declared would happen.

So fuck 'em
if they question your loyalty.
It never mattered anyway.
The grave
is the most silent place for critics.
They were only alive
when they convinced us
they were devoted.

She's terrible — but I want more.

Flying Without Feathers

People want to be witnessed,
but influencing the masses remains a stand-alone concept.
Doesn't a true connection sting harder than any needle?
When a cool breeze lifts the hairs of your arm.
A chill, so raw, that it scars.
A flaw so authentic you can kiss it.

And when you find that person,
the chaos of the world slows.
The flashes of inadequacy vanish.
Sky and faces glow red with fire,
and purpose presents itself.

Our life becomes theirs to witness.
They pace through life,
yearning for someone to see their greatness.
The depth of our bond remains a mystery to them.

I fly.
I for you.
I fly without feathers.

More Alive Than Birth

Nothing is alive
when it's cleaned up.

The smears on our face
wiped away by expectation.
And after it's wiped away,
we become the expected—
the cookie-cutter life
that snuffs the lively nature
of what could or would be.

We want to be useful,
so we abide.
But we trade desire—
what we once wanted disappears.

And in the tattered places around the world,
the liquor,
the drugs,
the sex workers—
they aren't in any despair.
They might say so.
But they live in the lively bliss
of freedom.
Of chance and wonder.
Of triumph and letdown.
Of brevity and burn.

As liars who believe in their schemes—
because often they fail,
but every once in a while
it works out.
And when it does,
it's more alive than your moment of birth.
Because even birth was expected.

But the chances thereafter?
All up to fate.

Most of life doesn't need to be explained,
simply its description suffices for our rationale.

So the racket of life keeps us going,
a turbulence we bleed for.

Where we can learn something new.
Where we can meet someone new.
Where we can change into something new.

To the onlookers,
in the safe places you live—
it's safe there.
But it's just there.
It'll never be more
than what it's structured to be.
It's your last place,
done in.

There will be nothing else
other than death.
And even that
will be
expected.

Run, wild one, run.

Steel Oats

Without vulgarity,
how could the obedient man
turn from compromise
to define himself by contradiction?

When working-class ruin
turns to spiritual rebellion,
you learn the cruelest truth—
safety kills the soul
long before struggle does.

Syrup Trickles Sideways

Men grow up to be gods or ghouls.
Region plays its part in that decision.

Some know places where men collect pallets for a few bucks,
curse under their breath,
and talk only about things
they can fix with their hands.

Others learn to collect fees for more bucks,
curse only in their minds,
and talk about nothing that can't be fixed
by the guy who collects pallets.

Few of us ever move on from soil made of
soot, sugar, and spirit.
It's there you earn rhythm from conveyor belts
and compassion from exhaustion.

Unbeknownst to us,
other kids were calculating stats,
moving through life by metric calibration.

Even when we get close to that world,
we can't shake our instinct—
the ability to measure emotion.
We know how anger moves through a room,
how silence stretches between sentences,
how love can sound like a slammed door.

This leaves a man lost in new settings—
tugged between stability and self-sabotage,
caught at the crossroads of convention and conviction.
Most men age and look back,
while others keep going forward.

We volunteer that weight.

A friction between order and upheaval,
between ambition and collapse.
It reeks of subway steam and rain-slick eulogies,
of sweat turned into sips of syntax.

Every line feels earned—
paid in the late-night rent of solitude.

There's a fine line
between the tortured genius
and the tortured common man.
Both pay bills,
wipe their asses,
and hope to hell they don't kill themselves.

Rarely does a man carry both sensitivity and intensity—
bruised knuckles, bruised heart,
but still swinging.

We're the best thing, the worst thing—
self-made, self-haunted, self-aware.

What you don't see is our fear:
that chase for something
always darting just out of reach:
truth, meaning, maybe redemption.
Still, we pulse with that pursuit—
equal parts rebellion and renewal,
uneven parts decay and defiance.

But we don't fucking posture.

We refuse your game.
We live the kind of life
most people are still pretending to write about.
Part outlaw. Part philosopher.
We move through the world
like men allergic to permission,
bleeding honesty into every decision
until it hurts just right.

And it falls like maple syrup—
sideways, at a trickle.
Nothing to be admired,
but enough to stay alive.

And when you meet us,
you feel that too—
the smoke, the grit, the hunger, the ache.

Proof your metrics never meant much—
there are still men who measure life by what they feel,
not what they earn.

It's not art. It's survival.
The chaos never left us.
We just learned how to make it sing.

Toward truth, not performance.
Toward presence, not applause.

Gun

Even bullets brace themselves
before charging through a barrel.

A gun gives.
A gun takes.

Take your shot.

A taste of destruction
has the perfect amount of disruption.

Cake Without Icing

Let's stop bragging
about what we bought,
what we saw.
What we ate, what we consumed.

Let's talk instead
about what you created,
wrote, built—
anything other than
the malware dictating our lives,
a commercial product,
an alibi for an algorithm.

We snort information like cocaine,
a high built on ads,
targeted marketing,
revivals of renditions—
a manufactured process
of faux superiority.

A basic bitch,
a basic bro,
a grey vest stamped with
a bank's logo.
Khakis—fucking khakis.
Pants like paper bags
vacuumed to skinny legs.

When did we become
so dull, so predictable,
so arrogant to the fact
that we're boring?

Sophistication has rotted
our curiosity.
Too safe, too cautious,
too weary to even care.
But no one is aware.

A simulation for followers,
the adopters of now,
the troubadours of commonality.

And there's no icing on their cake.
It's just cake—
spongy, maybe,
moist, never—
so dry.

Staged for us to admire.

If it looks real,
it must taste real.
But it isn't.
It's the nothingness we live for.
Some erroneous fabrication,
smeared across our livestream.

I'd rather make my own cake,
from scratch—
and eat it whole.

Wouldn't you?

This Land, This Motion

Through the train's electric cables
America exposes herself.

Marshes mix with rails,
workers hammer bolts,
blue-collar eyes deepen—watching
as passengers whoosh by.

There's an uncommon calmness in it,
a distant view of everyday chaos.
Time slows
as the train captures pictures for us.

Compact cars look like ladybugs,
4x4s crawl like beetles.
Closer and closer,
we near—
ready to squash them.
But it never happens.

The overpass saves them again.

Soccer fields. Cranes. Boarded-up apartments.
Run-down gas stations. Debris-strewn backyards.
Metal upon scrap metal,
mountains of sand,
fields of overgrown brush.
And look, a plane.

At the next stop, people sit on benches—
conversations of wonder:
"Is this the right track?"
"Did I miss the train?"
"It must be five minutes late."

Life waits.
Life moves.
Life happens.

And as I ride, I watch
the mundane routine, speckled like cars in a parking garage—
the same in,
the same out,
a stamp on a ticket,
another day done.
A reminder
to believe in tomorrow.

And I believe.
I believe in the endless landscape built on virtue.
The thought that if it hasn't happened,
it might.
And as long as we keep moving,
it might.

In the wistful beauty of possibility,
I believe in everyone out there.
I believe in their hopes and fears.

I believe this land is our land.

The heart cannot shield itself from being touched.

Grumbling Empire

New York is a beast,
but it's ours to ride.

A city of harsh takeovers,
spits in your eye,
blindsides that leave you ripped—
bleeding, vacant.

Dropped to exhaustion's edge,
you still crave more.

The streets are littered
with the ones who didn't make it.
Advertisements scream:
your face could be on it,
your name could be called.

You.
You can make it here.
You can make it anywhere.

And if that's not okay,
get the fuck out.

Because New Yorkers—
the hustlers,
the movers, the shakers,
the tireless campaigners in pursuit—
they know the city sleeps
only for those who've made it.

I know you're awake.
You know
you can't sleep yet.

The stream's endurance
lasts as long
as its dream flows.

Crawlers of the Night

On the outskirts of town,
from 2 a.m. to 5 a.m.,
the night crawls.

Sometimes I walk then,
taking a break from whatever I'm doing.
I never know why I'm up so late—
but that's beside the point.

I see them.
Not the spoiled ones
spilling money in clubs,
stirring disruption.

No.
I mean the crawlers of the night:
the street sweepers,
the trash men,
the subway crews.

A tight crew,
bonded by neon vests,
soap and suds,
musty trash,
lanterns and tired eyes.

The crawlers keep the city moving.
No thank-you necessary.
But when I walk, I try to catch their eyes.
They'll stare back, embarrassed at first,
though there's nothing to be ashamed of.
Like runners passing,
I give a nod.

The street steams with what could be.
Then morning rises,
erasing their work,
the city pretending to be self-sufficient.

Everyone goes about their day.
Nothing to thank.
Nothing to say.

Everything just as it was yesterday.
Just as the crawlers made it.
Just as the night crawls.

She is the wind,
impossible to control.

Burberry Goddess Eau de Parfum

When you find someone who makes you miserable,
who keeps you sleepless and raw,
yet happier than you've ever been,
you know it's rare.
You know it won't last forever.
But you gamble anyway.

Because you've lived with *fine*—
and *fine* is death.
Better to ache,
better to unravel,
than settle.
I wasn't mad
that she let me kiss her cheek at the subway—
I was sad.
Because yesterday it was her lips.
And I never thought such a stupid, trivial thing
could matter so much.

No plan prepares you
for the end,
for the smallest moments
that last longest.
To walk her to the train,
to even kiss her cheek,
to say goodbye—
that was privilege.

Her strength never wavered—
built out of each scar,
she grew from each failure.
I envied her.
She was a celebration,
the kind of love that ruins you.

A man's life is ruined without her.
A man's life is ruined with her.
A man's life is ruined by love.

Once,
I dreamed of mornings with coffee and eggs,
of fall walks with the dog,
of afternoons that slipped into winter light.
Simple looks.
One more.
And another.
And another.

But the heart breaks.
That stubborn organ—
giving life to the body,
still collapses under its own emptiness.
No logic explains it.
No certainty saves it.
Nothing guaranteed.
Everything to lose.
She deserves someone great.
So now I must be great.

Even if the ghost of her lingers,
fragrance leaves a man marked.

I'll remember her by Burberry.

They don't add to the cup of culture.
They sip from it, then spit critique.
Consumerism, corruption, cheap attention—
that's their legacy.

Infinity's First Time

And we change.
It's difficult to accept—
not the change itself,
but the urge to keep up with it,
the desire to hold on to an identity.

But identity reinvents.
It sways with climate,
with people,
with place.

We yearn for solace,
yet are planted in chaos—
doomed by the city's virtue,
stern as stone.

Sometimes desire turns real,
and desperation cracks the moment—
more than you can bear.
The rush of emotion bottled too long—
poured out,
spilled over,
scaring you with its flood.

You're not used to it.
There's nothing to do.
It's the first time—
until the next time—
that you touch infinity.

Alphabet Soup

Actions against anarchists annihilate auspicious arousal around arrogance.

Booty-bouncing businesses benefit balloon-blowing bourgeois.

Chaos controls catty cleavages.

Deliberate doppelgängers destroy defined destinies.

Eccentrics excavate extravagant elusions.

Frivolous follies flop, fantastic fixtures formulating false, fucking figments.

Ghastly giants grandiosely gravitate toward graveling graves.

Hysterical hindrance hides hollow homies.

Ignite ignoramus inside inspirational idiots.

Jetting juxtapositions jump justly.

Kindred ketchup keeps kitchens keen.

Lost lives lurk.

Morons mesmerize, mistakes made more maliciously—mirroring media's meager, meandering manifestations.

Nugatory nuisances neglect natural necessity, nudging nomads near Neanderthals.

Oppression occurs once opponents operate obstinately.

Persistent pushes pericardium pressure.

Quirky qualms quiver quickly, questioning quintessential quacks.

Rich rivals rarely rank reasonable remonstrations.

Soluble solutions stumble starkly.

Tumult tiptoes tepidly, taking terrible thoughts.

Underwear unveils universal utopian understanding.

Valuables vex vulnerable voices vapidly.

Wizards woo wretched women.

Xerox xenial xenophiles.

Yearning youth yak yellow.

Zesty zoos zestfully zigzag zygotes.

All the little ways you hunt to save money
are never worth the time it takes to find them.

Pay.
For.
Convenience.

I Stand

Cut me down.
Mislead me.
Trip me while I walk.
I will stand.

Years of focus.
Years of striving.
Years of failure.
I will stand.

In the crowd.
Out of the crowd.
Alone with silence.
I will stand.

Doubted.
Doubting myself.
Misled by doubt.
I will stand.

So heavy my legs betray me,
so drained my mind turns numb.
I whisper—I can't stand.

Depressed.
Deprived.
Mortified.
Defeated.

I crouch, collapse—nearly gone.
But I rise.
I stand.

Rebuild.
Revive.
Rise.

I must stand.
Not because they told me to.
Not because I pretend to.
But because the mirror leaves no choice.

Others say sit.
No.
I stand.

Because I dare.
Because life is my own.
Because sitting is nothing.

I stand for me.
I stand for you.
I stand.

Fathom the Fool

People claim they want authority,
but give them the weight of choice,
and they lean on the permission of others—
software, systems,
or those in positions of power.

To neglect accountability
is not reason,
even if others call it retreat.

Most can't fathom being seen the fool.
Blame terrifies them.
They dodge it
like lightning dodges ground,
shifting fault faster than thought,
pretending they wish they hadn't.

But inside—
they're relieved.
Relieved to surrender intent.
Relieved to stay unseen.

It's in this surrender
that most live without integrity,
passing over the chance
to make something of themselves,
all in pure fear
of their own vanity—
a phobia of exposure.

The cruelest cowardice.
The faint of heart,
fearing their own awakening.

Do you have fire in your heart,
or smoke in your head?

We Left No Relics

No relic was ever remembered for mere existence.
We've become gimmicks and critics—consuming, consuming, consuming.
We latch onto our take on things, malingering in the space between
what we think represents us,
but certainly isn't who we really are.

We so desperately want people to listen to us—
to say we are in the right,
even when we muddle what it is
we want from ourselves.

Our restraint isn't strength.
It's obedience.
And for that—we expect reward.
When that reward doesn't arrive, we seek vengeance—
for reasons we've already forgotten,
reasons that long ago stole our sense of self.

Our soul meets the price tag, the comment, the like.
We become narrowed-down versions of ourselves,
decisively vacant of moisture.
We misfire what we thought was right,
and dry up with faux importance—
indignant that what is must be right,
even as we relapse into former theory
and recall the glitter of truth.

Even that truth can stir a scuttle of facts,
each one backtracking toward the essential present—
not with servitude, but with anticipatory dread.
The pieces of our life aligned in some forced order
that refuses chaos.

But some sort of chaos is what we must live for.

How else can we open the caveats of the mind
to something new, fresh, undiscovered,
unbetrayed—unbeknownst even to the basic fibers

of blood, veins, and a heart
still pumping for whatever it is we need.

And we don't need to know what that is.
We don't need to know.
We don't need it.
We don't need all the things
we hope will spontaneously make something happen.

All we need is the mind to seek—
to seek more growth,
to seek more experience,
to seek the changeless liberty of carefree ways
that once made us hopeful—
not of the future,
but of now.
Then.
And whatever came before us.

With a steady stream of desire,
we can go so far as to seem unviable
to the rest of the world.

But maybe that's the point.
To live so vividly we leave no relic—
just rumors.
To disappear not from failure,
but from having burned too brightly to archive.

Because the future doesn't remember what merely survived.
It only remembers what dared to be.

Life dries
as fast as paint on a wall,
and moves
as slowly as an escalator.

Mistaken for a Heartbeat

It feels suspect
meeting someone
with a past too close to yours.

Impostors impose themselves
on the soul's raw vulnerability,
laced with the rush of unity.
Nothing feels stronger.

Pressure points pinch
in fierce determination.
A fleeting scream
scorches the spirit.

Windswept delusion
provokes the ache of loneliness—
until the wave crashes,
spun by a turbulent mind,
mistaken for a heartbeat.

A living tragedy,
gone again—
back to solitary.

Never again.

Write Like Hell

You write better
when you stop censoring yourself.

So live a little.
Study experience.
Pace yourself.
Refine your craft.

And when it stops feeling like work,
say whatever the fuck you want.

The Brutal Bugle

When the quit of life strums its chord,
we play the song of brutality.
No other melody will do.

Our filters clear;
the bugle of resentment blows.
The sparrow of strife sings.

We are unhappy with ourselves.
We are unhappy with others.
We are unhappy together.

Still we sing in unison—
a harmony of mockery,
a choir of whispers behind backs.

Because nothing stings more
than seeing your own reflection—
and finding it unbearable.

Young Company

I surround myself with young company
to forget about my fragility.
Aging isn't something I fear;
it's the effects of age that worry me.
I'm scared I'll forget what it's like to be fresh.
So I surround myself with young company.

They aren't transfixed by unrest.
There's ambition inside their souls.
They haven't been let down enough to feel guilt.
There's an inert community,
and they float as seamlessly as clouds in the sky—
adjacent to the vibrant blue,
white wisps of pure innocence.

I'm pushing forty.
My hair has thinned.
Hell, I know I'll lose it all soon.
My gut widens more quickly than it used to;
the hangovers last longer than a day—
yet this doesn't cross the minds of young company.

Although they may joke about my age,
and even if I look like the creepy guy
who needs to grow up,
they know it's different.
They see it in my eyes—
the fearless delusion of a man pressing on,
refusing to let the world get to him.

When I see the change in their eyes—
typically when least expected—
when the quit overtakes the fight,
when the howlers stop howling—
that's when I have to find new company.
I can't be around anything else.
I can't.
I just can't.

I'll always be around the young.
I live off their fervor for chaos.

I struggle to be more calculated,
because even with my wisdom,
I still get caught up in their unruliness—
for which their naivety excuses them.
Sometimes, even when I know
I should abide by society's rules,
I trick myself—wanting to feel
a sense of invincibility again.

I let myself believe.
Otherwise, there'd be very little left.
I'd become like those people who look back,
who decide those times have passed.
Reminiscent.
You wouldn't want to be around if that happened.
You couldn't bear the sight of my saddest eyes.

So I hold on.
The thrill of discovery outweighs
reaching the final destination.
And that's why I find myself
in young company.

The story never ends.

Hell in Her Blood

I haven't been in love lately.

Maybe all my love's been used up.
Too many women.
I'm not as taken as I was before—
when lustful firefields burned in my belly.

My passion feels cursory now—
older than the years when I'd throw it away.
I miss that recklessness.
I'd give it again if I could.

Maybe I'm in a season of waiting.
The wait's a burden,
but it's the only way to weigh the options.

The gaps between moments
turn into memories—
what I had once,
what I lost,
what I might find again.

I still fool around.
The young girls are carefree—
hell in their blood,
hornier than a devil in heaven.

But it doesn't excite me the same.
Maybe because I already know
what happens over time
to their crop.

At first, they're like corn in its husk—
golden-white, then turning yellow,
vibrant, beaming.

Once plucked, the energy fades.
Routine trickles in.
The corn turns brown,
brittle,
bored.

That's when I throw it away.
I don't want it anymore—
and neither do they.

So I wait.
Next season comes,
whether I want it or not.

I always wait.

Some Sort of Chaos

The summer had been dull.
It was everything all over again.
Then came a chance encounter.

She was younger—
fifteen years below me.
But I was an old catcher's mitt—
worn, rugged,
ready for another throw.

I needed it.
She needed it.
We didn't know until we felt it.

A stagnant mind
always needs a good fuck.

Without it,
the brain's just loose circuitry—
electricity waiting for a lamp.

Always searching for something.
Always looking to be turned on.

The burden of life runs
in currents of nostalgia.
So when a spark comes,
burst the bulb—
it's the iron inside we're seeking,
not the illumination.

We fucked.
We bent the rules.
She screamed for it
over and over.
That's the pain of pleasure.
That's the rush of release.
That's the break of motion.

Sex—like drugs—
gives us an identity crisis.

Every now and then you need some smut.
Carnal craving reminds us of humanity.
A mind opened against the common current—
it shows us the person we are... isn't.
And maybe that means
we can be someone else.

Because if you don't feed yourself,
you'll starve from
deprivation,
dismissal,
or a dead dick.

We didn't starve.
We didn't defend.
We just went again.
This time more slowly.

The cock, stiff with consequence.
Her swallow—rich, like a delta.
And the rock slid
through the cascade of her sand.
It was silk—
a slide of euphoria.
And we each throbbed
a little more,
a little hotter,
a little brighter,
until the rock
crumbled
into
mud.

Then we lay there—
across the plains.
We were back to normal,
until we overthought it.
But for now we don't.
Why ruin
some sort of chaos?

Most people go before they look
and wonder why they crash.

Photo: Sasha Kay

The Author

Joseph Adam Lee is a Franco-American poet and writer from Lewiston, Maine, where factory smoke and river light first taught him the rhythm of poetry. Each line he writes feels lived-in, unapologetic, and electric with self-interrogation. His work stands as a portrait of a man wrestling with meaning in an age of performance.

He lives in New York City.

Contact Information

Email: joe@therebelwithin.com
Website: www.josephadamlee.com
Instagram: @joseph.adam.lee

Letters & Packages

Red Fox Runs Press
C/O Joseph Adam Lee
909 3rd Avenue
#127
New York, New York 10150

www.ingramcontent.com/pod-product-compliance
Lightning Source LLC
LaVergne TN
LVHW091134080826
845145LV00008B/2154

* 9 7 8 1 9 4 6 6 7 3 4 4 2 *